# WE
## THE PEOPLE
# JIM BRIDGER

Published by Creative Education, Inc. 123 South
Broad Street, Mankato, Minnesota 56001

**Library of Congress Cataloging-in-Publication Data**

Zadra, Dan.
  Jim Bridger : the mountain man (1804-1881) / Dan Zadra ;
illustrated by Nancy Inderieden.

   p. cm. — (We the people)
  Summary: A brief biography of the nineteenth-century trapper,
scout, and explorer who helped open the West to settlers.
  ISBN 0-88682-179-7
  1. Bridger, Jim, 1804-1881—Juvenile literature.   2. Pioneers—
West (U.S.)—Biography—Juvenile literature.   3. Frontier and
pioneer life—West (U.S.)—Juvenile literature.   4. West (U.S.)—
Biography—Juvenile literature.   [1. Bridger, Jim, 1804-1881.
2. West (U.S.)—Biography.   3. Frontier and pioneer life—
Biography.]   I. Inderieden, Nancy, ill.   II. Title.   III. Series:
We the people (Mankato, Minn.)
F592.B85Z33   1988
978'.02'0924—dc19
[B]
[92]                                                          87-36473
                                                                CIP
                                                                 AC

# WE
# THE PEOPLE
# JIM BRIDGER

## THE MOUNTAIN MAN
## (1804-1881)

DAN ZADRA

Illustrated By Nancy Inderieden

CREATIVE EDUCATION

## *WE THE PEOPLE*
# *JIM BRIDGER*

Jim Bridger has been called, "the Daniel Boone of the Rocky Mountains." Like Boone, Bridger was an early American explorer, trader and scout. Boone may be the most famous of the two men. But Bridger was probably tougher, braver and more reckless. Yes, Jim Bridger was a true "mountain man," and this is his story.

Jim was born in Richmond, Vir-

upstream for 1,800 miles, with hostile Indians lining the shore most of the way.

At the mouth of the Yellowstone River they built a log stockade. It was named Fort Henry. This would be headquarters for the fur trappers, who would range out in all directions seeking the valuable beaver fur.

Jim learned the trade of a mountain man—as the fur trappers were called. He lived outdoors for months on end in all kinds of weather. At night he slept under the open sky. His food was wild game, his drink cold water, and his best friend a buffalo rifle. Always there were the Indians, ready to raid or take his scalp.

Jim learned to love the high country. He made numerous expedi-

tions in mountainous areas of Montana, Idaho, Wyoming, Utah and the Dakotas. Often, he and his horse would climb all day to reach a new pass between peaks. There, he would stop and gaze down on the other side. It was thrilling to know that he was probably the first white man to see what he was seeing.

In 1824, Jim went with a famous trailblazer, Jedediah Smith, and some other men. They were the first to cross the South Pass through the Rockies from east to west. The path they made would later become part of the great Oregon Trail. It would open the Northwest to thousands of settlers.

In 1825, Jim made a discovery that turned him into a legend among his fellow mountain men. It seems that Jim and some trappers were camped in Indian country along the Bear River. They wondered where the river went.

"I'll find out!" said young Jim Bridger.

He built himself a bull-boat. First he made a frame out of strong saplings. It was shaped like a large bowl. Then he stretched and sewed buffalo hide over the frame. "You're crazy,

Jim!" the men said. "What if you go over a waterfall?"

But Jim only grinned. He cut a long pole, got into his boat, and sailed fearlessly down the river.

Then he entered the rapids.

The tiny boat whirled through foaming water, crashing into rocks and bouncing off canyon walls. Jim hung on for his life and wondered if he should jump out. At last the river calmed down. After passing through an eerie marsh, Jim emerged on a tremendous body of water. He tasted it—and it was salty.

"It's the Pacific Ocean!" he exclaimed. But he was wrong. Jim Bridger had discovered Utah's Great Salt Lake, until then a secret known only to the Indians.

City-slickers in the East scoffed when they heard that a mountain man named Jim Bridger had discovered a 2,000-square-mile salt lake. "Ridiculous," they said. Then Jim explored the strange country that would one day become Yellowstone Park. He sent back tales of weird petrified forests, bubbling hot springs, boiling mudholes and steaming geysers. For a long time, these reports were branded as "Jim Bridger's lies." When they were finally verified as true, the legend of Jim Bridger spread far and wide.

Now, the leaders of the most important Western exploring expeditions all wanted the famous Jim Bridger to be their guide. He became known even among the Indians for

his honesty and bravery.

In 1832, Jim guided an expedition for Benjamin Bonneville, an important U.S. Army explorer. There was a fight with Blackfoot Indians and Jim was shot in the back with two arrows. One of them remained in his tough body for two years—until it was removed by the pioneer missionary-surgeon, Dr. Marcus Whitman, who was on his way to Oregon.

Mountain men like Jim Bridger built no homes and tilled no farms. Beaver pelts were their money. They lived like Indians—and many of the western tribes were friendly to them. In 1835, Jim married the daughter of a Flathead chief.

But times were changing. After years of trapping, the beaver were be-

In 1843, Jim and a partner built
Fort Bridger in southwest Wyoming
to supply the settlers traveling on the
Oregon Trail. It was a great success.
Many pioneers passed through it and

24

were helped by Jim. In 1847, he advised Brigham Young, leader of the Mormons, about fertile lands that lay in Utah. The Mormons followed Jim's advice and settled south of the Great Salt Lake he had explored.

Jim knew personal tragedy during those years. His first wife died, and so did his second. He then married Little Fawn, daughter of the Shoshoni chief, Washakie.

In 1850, Utah became a territory of the United States. Brigham Young was its governor. The people of Utah needed money, and Young decided to take over Fort Bridger. Jim was ordered to turn the fort over to new managers. He refused, and Fort Bridger was burned!

Betrayed and brokenhearted, Jim

began—so fantastic had been his life. When Jim Bridger died in 1881, the West was all but tamed.

Today, Fort Bridger has been set aside forever as a state park—a place of natural beauty that would surely bring a smile to a mountain man's face.